# UNCLE B. PUBLICATIONS

## INDIANAPOLIS

# Doughnut Shaded Sunsets

A Collection of Poetry

John Kojak

Doughnut Shaded Sunsets

First Printing, September 2022

©2022 by John Kojak

unclebpublications@gmail.com

ISBN: 978-1-957034-15-7

# Table of Contents

*For Elizabeth*

*The queen of madness; I worship at your feet.*

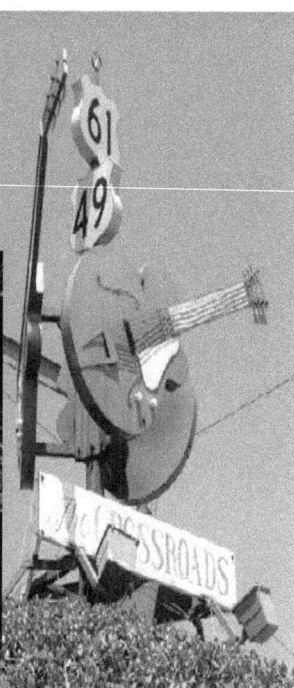

*Part 1*

## Bukowski's Bungalow

I was on my way out of L.A.

but I couldn't leave town yet,

there was one final stop I had to make.

I knew I was close when I saw

a beat-up bar with boarded up windows

and graffiti scrawled walls

across the street from a liquor store.

This had to be the place,

I could smell the stale cigars

and taste the cheap wine…

I slowed the car down

and turned left off Sunset Boulevard

onto Normandie Avenue,

then made a quick right onto De Longpre.

There was an old red Toyota Corolla

sitting in the middle of the road

with its hazard lights on.

A large muscled, brown-skinned man

with long, straight black hair

was kneeling on the smoldering asphalt

next to the left front tire.

He had the spare tire propped up

against the fender

and gave me a long—hard look

as I drove slowly by.

His eyes said I shouldn't be there,

they said this was his neighborhood,

his street. His fucking world...

But he was wrong.

It was, and now forever will be,

Charles Bukowski's.

I know this because there is a sign on the pole

in front of the low-slung adobe walled bungalows

at 5124 De Longpre Avenue

that says this place, Bukowski's place,

is a cultural heritage site.

I think that Hank, as he was known

to the prostitutes

and lowlifes of East Hollywood,

would get a kick out of that.

After all, this this is where he spent his wild years,

3

his Linda King years.

This is where the young blondes in stiletto heels

stumbled up crumbling sidewalks

and over shattered whiskey bottles

in the hopes that this beaten,

broken old man

might mount them, thrusting his

flaccid purple penis inside them

until he made it, or he didn't.

That never seemed to matter to Hank.

He was too surprised to be on top of them

in the first place.

You see, writers don't get the good stuff.

They get the broken ones,

the ones desperate for feelings,

any kind of feelings at all,

and only the most desperate of those,

only the lowest of the breed,

will fuck a poet.

*Only the desperate,* I thought

as I peered into the small side window

of the worn-out old bungalow

hoping to get a glimpse of some piece of him,

an ancient reflection—a shadow.

Anything.

It had been over forty years

since he wrote, since he drank, since he fucked here,

yet there I was.

A desperate, third-rate hack

in search of inspiration,

any kind of inspiration at all,

because I am truly the lowest of the breed.

I am a poet.

## The Poet

To hell with words

I eat them like sushi

And cast their bones

In the street

Next to the Dali Lama

Diarrhea Diatribes

And switchblade

Jizz-saws

Cut on, cut up,

And torn open

I killed

the Lizard King

Let's go

Up to my room

Eat elderberry pies

And drink some jinn

Put the lizard

In the blender

And do it again

## Strange Days

I was standing outside Bukowski's

old place on De Longpre Avenue

—I think I mentioned that already,

but I didn't tell you what happened

when I turned around to leave...

There was a homeless man

riding a shopping cart

down the steep slopped street

like a dopped up dog sled racer.

He had one foot on the back axel,

while his other leg was stuck out behind him

like a pirouetting figure skater.

He held onto the handle with both hands,

and leaned forward over the basket

so the whole thing wouldn't tip over.

He was wearing a long, worn trench coat and gray scarf

and screaming "Weeeeeeeee" at the top of his lungs

as he flew gleefully down the street toward the resurrection.

I have seen a lot of strange shit in L.A.

but that was definitely the strangest...

I stood there for a minute after he passed

wondering what Hank would have thought about it.

I can't really say,

but I am pretty sure

he would have written a poem about it.

## *Poesy*

I write at dawn

When there are no stars

And the morning stinks

Of whiskey

My pen wandering

Like a stray dog

Down a dead-end street

# *Tex*

The story was good.

There was a one-legged hooker,

piles of cocaine,

and guns—lots of guns.

I liked it.

The only problem I had with it

was that the tale took place down by the border

in Texas,

and the main character was called Tex.

Nobody calls you Tex—when you're in Texas.

Now, if you're from Texas,

and go to say, Montana

and someone ask you where you're from

—and you say Texas,

well, then they might call you Tex.

But you can't go back to Texas

and tell people your name is Tex.

They would laugh in your face,

kick your ass,

or both.

I told the young writer this,

and that it was probably why

the story kept getting rejected.

But the kid just stared blankly back at me

and said that that was only my opinion

and he wasn't going to change it.

He was from California,

I'm from Texas.

I thought about punching his teeth in

just on general principal,

but in the end, it was his story

and you should always write *your* story,

not someone else's.

But—there is always a but,

when someone who knows

tells you how it is

that is a different thing entirely.

Now, I know I don't know everything,

especially about writing,

but I am sure of two things.

That writer's character is still called Tex,

and his story is still unpublished.

## *Getting Published*

Getting published is hard.

First there is the writing.

Which, like any craft demands a certain level

of natural skill combined with years of astute learning

and meticulous assembly.

Then the re-writing, and the re-writing,

and the re-writing.

And then,

when you finally think you have produced something

of any value at all

there is the submitting, and the re-submitting,

and the rejections,

and the submitting and rejections,

and the rejections (Did I mention the rejections?).

It's tough,

you need a lot of faith in yourself to see it through.

To keep pounding away on that keyboard.

To keep hitting send—send—send

until some brilliant publisher

(And they must be brilliant,

because they were able to see the true genius

in your work when the other fools could not.)

accepts your short story or poem for publication

in their inevitably small, independent literary magazine.

If you're lucky, they might send you a buck or two.

Maybe even enough for a cup of coffee at Starbucks

—as long as you don't get carried away, and order

a Caramel Macchiato Latte.

## The Girl in The Wheelchair

Writer's groups are often thought of as safe spaces

where writers of all shapes, sizes, skill, and education levels

can come out of their dark, solitary caves and gather

for a circle-jerk of mutual praise and adulation.

It can be helpful for the spirit, but seldom for the writing.

Mostly because no one tells you what you really need to hear,

which is—that you suck.

And that's okay, for the most part.

It's hard to look into the eyes of a young mother, or recent widow

or widower (There are always a lot of those.), and tell them

the truth—that not everyone can or should be a writer.

But there are times when I have been surprised.

Gob smacked,

by someone who I had written off in my mind

as a self-publishing poser or psych-ward wannabe.

The girl in the wheelchair was one of those...

The group that night was meeting in a coffee shop.

There were a half-dozen or so of us out on the patio when she arrived.

We watched as her mother unloaded her from one of those vans

with the hydraulic lifts on the side, it was impressive.

15

The girl was on the ground and zooming toward us in no time,

and you could see the pride on her mother's face.

Her little princess was growing up—putting herself out there,

and the girl, just a teenager, was beaming.

This was a big deal.

She was stuck in that chair, but she wasn't going to let

her disabilities define her—she was a writer *damnit!*

And tonight she would share her work with her peers,

and we would see the same genius and potential in her words

that her mother and friends saw.

And we all wanted to—or at least say we did.

These writer meetups are mostly bullshit,

but you could tell that everyone there that night

wanted to give the young girl as much

support and encouragement that we possibly could.

Once the readings started,

the group went through the normal motions,

giving the same perfunctory punctuation corrections

and vanilla character and plot observations as always

while we all waited to read *her* story.

And, when we did, it was good—very good.

Her characters were smart and the plot was interesting,

and she incorporated social media into her writing

in unique and clever ways.

She was talented, and we all told her so.

And she was happy—really happy.

It was a moment.

That night changed how I think about those meetings.

Maybe we aren't just there to jerk each other off.

Maybe it's about being human, and sharing not just our work

but little pieces of ourselves

with other humans.

I went to a few more meetups after that,

but I never saw the girl in the wheelchair again.

I hope she is still writing—I really do.

## *Ariel Lost*

She was writing a lot.

Some of her best work.

Some might even say,

she was really cooking

in that little apartment

(Yeats' old place)

in London,

during the coldest, dreariest

winter in a hundred years.

But that didn't seem to matter to her.

She had a new vein of heartache to mine,

even richer than the one her father left her.

She was writing furiously in the frigid rain.

Trying to warn us with her words.

Warn us about life,

and love, and betrayal.

But most of all,

she was trying to warn us about Ted Hughes.

And let us know what a colossal asshole he was...

She was not wrong.

## On The Subject

Has there ever been a bigger

piece of shit than Ted Hughes?

How many women have to

kill themselves

before you get the message?

One woman turning on the gas

is a tragedy, what does two

say about you—and she took

your daughter too!

But wait, some might argue,

he was a poet.

The Poet Laureate of England no less!

Well, of course he was…

English men in general,

and English poets in particular

are assholes.

Well, maybe not all of them.

I will give Keats a pass,

because he became a doctor

to treat people with tuberculosis

19

after his younger brother

died of the disease.

Then he contracted TB

and died from it himself. Props…

And Blake—he was next level.

A true OG anarchist.

And Oscar Wilde, that dude was cool.

And Lord Byron…

Reaching into Percy Shelly's

burning funeral pyre and

yanking out his dead friend's heart.

That is about as poetic as you can get.

So, I guess not *all* English

poets are assholes,

but Ted Hughes definitely was.

I mean, who else would think

destroying a woman meant you

owned her ashes—and her poetry too.

## *Poison Girl*

There is a bar in Montrose

called Poison Girl.

They have poetry readings there

on the last Thursday of every month.

I went there once, with a fresh poem

folded up in my back pocket.

The ink still wet,

my delusions laid out

on one eight-by-eleven

sheet of bonded white paper.

I got to the bar early, and ordered a

Maker's Mark on the rocks.

It was a good start. I sipped my whiskey

and stared at the lounge-lizard red walls

covered with black-velvet nude paintings

of large breasted amazon women.

I had been to worse,

(coffee shop readings are suicide holes).

The readings here took place in the back,

inside a colorfully lit courtyard beside

a life-size paper mache Kool Aid Man.

First up was an older woman

named Lilly. She read several poems

from a book she wrote about addiction.

The poems were good—not great,

but they stirred the small crowd

of over educated MFA students

and nose-ringed hipsters to applause.

Next up was a PHD candidate

from South Africa. He wasn't bad,

but you could sense the desperation.

I had heard him talking to a friend

at the bar earlier. He was working

on his first book of poetry,

his ticket to the big leagues.

His friend said it would surely make

him famous.

But his poems didn't receive

the same enthusiastic applause

as Lilly's had,

and you could see the literal horror

of the crowd's reaction on his face.

He was going places,

he just knew it,

it's a shame no one else did.

Several University of Houston

English Professors (bow-tied literazi)

held court over the readings,

and shuffled a few more poets,

and NPR types up to the stage.

Each one receiving a little less

applause than the ones before,

until the crowd began to move

back to the bar

where the real poetry is made.

I ordered another Maker's

and wondered what the crowd

would have thought about mine.

A little poem I wrote about

some kids who got massacred

at an elementary school

in Connecticut.

I am not saying it's great,

but it's real.

And that was something missing

from the posers and pretenders

that read that night.

I never took my poem

out of my pocket. But it is entitled

Forty Little Feets,

and you can find it within these pages,

if you are so inclined.

Have a drink, and if you have time,

let me know what you think.

## *Open Mic*

You step to the mic,

open your mouth,

and take from me.

I am lesser now,

my solace and serenity

shattered by your tepid verse.

The letters, arranged

so as not to offend, offend me.

Your cat died—your boyfriend left you,

or was it the other way around?

My poetic soul is under assault.

I want to murder myself,

I can only image how they felt.

Please stop, my mind is begging you.

It screams STOP!

But you continue…

## Terminal Lucidity

In their final moments of madness,

some poets may experience

a period of terminal lucidity

in which they realize

they were nothing more

than social masochists.

Idiots, posers, and pretenders

who waisted their lives

filling little red notebooks

full of insipid verse

in a desperate attempt

to prove they were different,

special in some way.

That their words, so arranged,

could cut a deeper wound

than the paintings of an elephant.

What fools.

## *Nothing*

Well, here I am—again

Sitting in front of a keyboard

Trying to create *SOMETHING*

Whose entire purpose is to entertain you


So, what'll it be?


A scary story?

Something funny?

How about a poem about that time I lost everything?

Or the girl I fucked in a train station in Japan?


No, no…that won't do


You want a show


But I am not going to cut an ear off

Or blow my brains out

Or stick my head in the oven

       Well, not for you anyway


I will simply give you this poem

For you to enjoy

Like a bag of soggy tacos

*Part 2*

## *Chinatown*

Memories of ex-lovers hang in my head

Like naked chickens

In the window of a Chinese restaurant

## Falling Down

I woke up last night in the middle of the day,

the Sunday sun seeping in through

broken blinds.

I reached for a half-empty beer on the dresser.

My head throbbing,

I looked over at the crumpled sheets.

The freckled white flesh was gone.

All that remained of her were

a pair of pretty pink panties falling down

over my old blue-jeans.

I lit a cigarette and coughed,

wishing I was still drunk or stoned,

before the loneliness crept in again.

In a week, I won't remember

The redhead, or her bright green eyes.

But I'll remember those pretty pink panties,

falling down.

## *The Drawer Beside The Bed*

One red Mickey Mouse t-shirt, worn

Two pairs of panties, one white, one blue

Three pairs of fuzzy socks, multi-colored

One pair of pink-pig purple pajama pants

       They are all that is left of you…

## *The Awkward Book*

An awkward book sat on the shelf

alone and untouched for many years,

yet its gilded pages called to me.


Unsure of the weight it carried,

I reached for it with cautious hands.

Careful not to crack its delicate spine,

I lovingly spread it open before me.


Delighting in its tight signatures,

I caressed each leaf as if they were

the fingers of a lover's hand.

But soon its shabby threads began to fray.


Fearful of damaging its frail bindings,

I hurriedly placed the awkward book

back on the shelf where it had sat.


I look for it now and then,

but it has somehow been misplaced.

Still, I reach for it.

33

## *Blockbuster*

On Friday nights

We would walk

The aisles

For what seemed

Like hours

Looking at all

The new releases

But after

We got home

We could never

Make it through

A whole movie

Not even one—ever

There was too much

Fucking to do

We could have

Bought a house

With the late fees

## *Our Love*

We rut like wild beast in the field

Our hips grinding the skies to dust

Twisting and twirling into purple

Our bodies bearing no relation to flesh

We fold like wildflowers in the wind

      As we realize our love is not like the earth

It bends in relation to morning

# *Christmas Morning*

I lay awake beside you

Waiting for your eyes to open

With the excitement of a child

On Christmas Morning

## *Metropolis*

You began as a fervent light

in the distance

Upon first glance,

a thing bright but minute

But I can see now that

you are no small thing

You are a colossus,

a giant sprawling metropolis

Replete with highways,

bi-ways, and busy streets

I like to wander through

their splendor and decay

Hoping to find the vibrant heart,

the main square

Where you will be waiting,

an answer to my prayer

## *Because of You*

*Not Even The Rain Has Such Small Hands*

—It's a line from an E.E. Cummings poem

That I have tattooed on my arm because of you

Because of you, because of you

Everything, because of you…

# A Few Things

There are a few things

Just a few things

I love about you

Like how

We can be together

When we are not

And how your eyes

Your eyes

Light up the world

And your feet

I love to rub your feet

—When you let me

And hold you tight at night

A call, a text

The sound of your voice

A heart emoji

On a fucked-up day

Your smile

These are just a few things

I love about you

But they are not everything

You, you are everything

# *Here in My Arms*

You lie gently, like a baby,

here in my arms

My hands firmly grasping

the world between them

Safe now and forever,

no one can do you any harm

The smile of sweet serenity

creases your lips

As you slip deeply

into the crevasses of my soul

Lie gentle baby,

here in my arms

There are so many things

that I still have to give you

But none more precious

than a simple kiss

Sleep softly baby,

no one can do you any harm

I doubt anyone anywhere

has ever loved like this

Even Cupid cries

when he sees our embrace

Safely forever now,

you lie gently

—here in my arms

## Picture Frame

An empty picture frame sits silent,

Its glass cold and dark

Leering like a shattered window,

Into the ruins of my heart

Gone are the memories,

Of love and joy it once contained

Now it's just an empty picture frame

To others it might seem perfectly fine

But not to me, or to myself,

Not when the memories gone are mine

## My Heart

There's a hole in my guitar

When I'm sad

I hide my heart inside

But it doesn't like it in there

It says it's too dark

I tell it to stop crying

But it won't

I give it scotch, wine, and

Whatever else I can find

But it doesn't care

It doesn't like it in there

Shut up!

She's not coming back, I say

Do you want her to fuck your shit?

There's another kind of box

I could put you in

Then we would both be dead, I tell it

But it doesn't care,

It doesn't like it in there…

## *Hey Baby*

I dreamed you came back to me

We held hands, and you told me
You loved me

But your eyes were different
So was your hair

Hell,
Maybe it wasn't you at all

## *Hello Darling*

I am alone in a house,

With a cat

Is this hell,

Darling where are you

Jasmine and lilacs

And shit in the streets

The world demands

Too much from me

Where do I

File the bombs

I must be sick,

Or insane,

With great big teeth

I can't sleep when

It's raining

It rains all the time

The news says

The bridges are all closed

How will I ever get out of here

## 2:32 a.m.

It's two thirty-two in the morning

Car alarms are wailing in the distance

And the neighbor's dog won't shut up

Somewhere metal is banging against metal

It's a conspiracy, the Illuminate are against me

My sanity comes and goes in silent waves

Through the darkness I see the end,

Or how it should be…

It was all a mistake, all of it

I rub my sallow crust, I count the bones

There is nothing left from the cradle

After her, there never was

## Road Trip

Abandoned, I drive west

leaving the urine-soaked streets

of New Orleans behind me.

My heart lost in the immense

darkness beyond the road.


I turn north onto Highway 61,

letting the waning glow of the

hallow moon guide me

toward the siren graves of

ancient agonies.


I can see the levees rising against me,

I can smell the sweet sweat of the cotton fields,

I can hear the bark of the hounds,

I can feel the whip, as it rips the flesh from my back.


The Mississippi Delta...

This is where the blues was born.

Where man forgot he was man,

and evil ruled so completely that even

Jesus was forced to look away.


Yet, I hope to find peace along the big river.

I hope to find solace among the echoes

of other lost souls.

## *Othello*

A handkerchief—

Ain't that the god-damn truth

Not that it was true in Othello's case,

But that is how women do you

You love them until you can't breathe

Then,

God-damn handkerchiefs

It's not that you're not a man,

You are

He was a general for Christ's sake

It's just the way they do you

The way they do all of us

## Matchbox Lovers

I used to play with matches when I was a kid

I still do, but now the boxes are full of women

Redheads, Brunettes, and Blonds

All ready to burn your house down

As soon as you rub them the wrong way

## *The Crazy Ones*

You know the ones I'm talking about...

They are usually

Tall and skinny

With long straight hair

That they brush a hundred times a day

They are a little awkward when they walk

And a little shy when they talk

But when their clothes are off

There is a wild sexuality about them

And they are always

ALWAYS

Great fucks

But there is something...

W r o n g

You don't know quite what

—at first

But the more they talk

The more you *know*

The Code says to leave

Run!

as soon as the crazy comes out

Because, if you don't

They will suck you in with their

Young, tight pussies

And never let you get away

## The Ex

I tried to call you—

but the message said

your line has been disconnected.

I tried to email you too, but Gmail

claims the email account doesn't exist.

Can you believe it!

I can't find your profiles on Facebook,

Twitter, or Instagram anymore either.

I tried to write you a letter,

but it came back a few weeks later

marked - Return to Sender.

I went by your apartment yesterday,

just to make sure the Post Office

hadn't made some kind of mistake.

You know how they are…

We used to laugh at the mailman

who wore those tight blue shorts,

do you remember?

No one answered your door,

but I was able to peak into a window.

Either someone stole your furniture, or

—I don't know what happened.

Did you move?

Why didn't you tell me?

I thought we were still friends...

You told me you would love me forever.

Do you remember that?

Or how you liked it when I played with your hair.

I called the police

and tried to report you as a missing person,

but the officer said I had to be a family member.

I tried to explain to him

that I am much more than that,

but the stupid cop wouldn't listen.

I will try going by your mother's house soon.

It's a long drive,

but hopefully she knows something.

If you read this poem before I find you,

*CALL ME!!!*

# Freedom

I am still here, still standing

But there are parts of me

That have been defeated

Beaten down and broken

By a never-ending river

Of ignorance, intolerance,

And hate

It's the stupidity of it all

Waking up

Expecting the day, any day

To be better

Free of the fools and liars

A day when trust isn't broken

And love isn't lost

I want to go back

To a time before everything

A time before I even existed

I would feel safe there

In the darkness

Free from it all

Free from you

*Part 3*

## Sweet Tea

When you grow up in The South

There are two things you are expected to do

Address your elders as sir and ma'am

And drink Sweet Tea

Simple rules for simple people

Folks

It is all about respect and belonging

Respecting your elders (the white ones)

Respecting the flag

No, not *that* one

The one that hangs in the back window

Of pickup trucks, behind the gunrack

The one that says the war is not over

It will never be over…

And belonging

Belonging to the great white race

Belonging to the southern patriarchy

The vast herd of exceedingly polite

Haters

Who sip their Sweet Tea, and wait

For the stars and bars to wave again…

## Don't Shoot!

Don't shoot!

Six shots

Brown down

Streets rise

Shields up

Gas flies

Chaos

Tanks

Machine guns

Is this America?

Get up

Speak out

We own this

We are Ferguson

I am Mike Brown

Don't shoot!

## The Pool

I learned to swim in a community pool

in Pasadena, Texas during the 1970's.

I didn't know it was a segregated pool.

I just knew it was where all the kids

went swimming in the summertime.


That is, until one summer when it was

wasn't. We would drive by and see the

empty pool, it gates locked, its water drained.

I asked my mother why, but she never said

anything that made any sense. At least to me.


It wasn't until I was much older,

that I learned the pool had been closed

because someone had sued, and the city

had been ordered to open the pool to everyone

Whites, Blacks, Hispanics, Asians, and Jews.


But the good folks of Pasadena had another

idea. Just shut it down. Equality through animus.

This was happening all over the south during

those days, and I bet there were a whole lot

of little kids like me who never understood why.


The worst part is, The Supreme Court

told them they could (1971 Palmer v

Thompson). The same court that just

decided (fifty years later), that women

cannot control their own bodies.

What the hell kind of world is this...

## *Coffee Beans*

Light Roast, Medium Roast, Dark Roast

Breakfast Blends, Classic, and French Roast

The beans are all the same

They are just roasted a little longer

—Why can't we see ourselves this way

## *Cheeto Mussolini*

There is something not quit right about you

It's the hue

The indigo orange glow

A Yellow #6 food dye

Colored shit stain

Covering your face like

Cheeto Bukkake

You see yourself as a modern-day Mussolini

A vile fascist Pied Piper

Leading a parade of brown-shirted

Neo-Nazi cuckolds

Down into the tyrannical abyss

Where are they now, Twittler?

After your failed rodeo clown revolution

Now even they have abandoned you

But I won't, I will follow you

All the way to your grave

   —And shit on it, BIGLY

## *White Jesus*

I am lucky—in a way

That my dark skin comes from

The Middle East

Not West Africa or South America

Thank God (the European one)

Jesus was Middle Eastern

That makes me white, with a tan

Instead of colored

Because we all know

Jesus could **never** be colored

## $$$

I have paid for sex. Oh lord, how I've paid...

## Skin Traders

The small ramshackle shacks

In Rose Mary's village crumbled like matchsticks

When the Typhoon hit

It was three weeks before the roads opened

And the men came

Not with fresh water, or food

But with money...

Rose Mary's mother held her baby brother Jacob in her arms

As she told Rose Mary that everything was going to be alright

That she was going to work for a rich family

That they would take care of her now

Her mother kept repeating the words

—Everything is going to be alright—

Pronouncing each word slowly and deliberately

As if she was trying to convince herself it was true

Her father stood in the kitchen doorway

Cigarette smoke swirling up

Through the collapsed roof above him

He said nothing, did nothing

As a strange man took her by the hand

And led her out to an old white van

Whose tires were worn from constant journey

66

# *Guapo*

I love you long time, no shit

That's what the Filipina

Girls used to say

When I was young

And handsome,

—And didn't give a shit

## *Shit River Bridge*

There was once a place

in the Philippines

called Shit River Bridge

that crossed a large drainage

ditch and connected the town

of Olongapo

to the U.S. Naval Base

in Subic Bay.

In the water beneath

the bridge,

were small boats filled

with little Filipina girls

who were too young

to work in the bars,

but not too young to eat.

They wore colorful dresses

and dove into the

shit-soaked river for coins.

Collecting the souls of

young drunken sailors,

five Pesos at a time.

*Part 4*

## Dreams

We don't meet our parents,

Until after their dreams have died.

Shattered upon incorporate rocks,

Drowned in seas of utopian debt.

Like gamboling babies,

They scream in the night.

# Father's Day

You hoped to hear the angels sing,

but there were none

Only the frozen gaze of horror

as you spied your ticket's gate

There was some joy in me of that,

payback

My heart as cold as your body blue

Into the earth or into the fire?

The worms squirmed hungrily for you,

but I couldn't deny the flames their due

Years passed,

and still your memory does not wane

The lingering stench of your spirits,

an eternal reminder of the pain

It's Father's Day!

Time to begin

I take off the lid,

scrape off the crust,

and burn you into ashes—again

## Goodbye

I didn't want to ride in the ambulance,

Or fill out the forms at the hospital

I definitely didn't want to see the body

Everyone says it's time to remember,

But all I want to do is forget…

## *The Day After*

The day after

I stood on a beach three thousand miles away,

while your body cooled on a cold steel slab.

Rays of drunken sunshine washed over me

as children ran screaming along the sandy shore,

their laughter-soaked innocence not yet betrayed

by the knowledge of death.

Desperate to escape the raging heat,

I buried my toes deep into the damp sand

and let the waves roll gently over my feet.

As I felt the water's cool release,

someone there pressed a button,

that ignited a spark,

that lit the flame.

Quickly you were gone from this place

(your big toes and oddly shaped head),

reduced to something less than a memory.

All that remains now are unwritten stories

and the tears of your daughter.

She cried beside your hospital bed.

She hasn't stopped.

73

## The Vodka Challenge

My uncle Howard drank himself to death

I was just a child at the time

But I remember when they found him

They said his whole house was filled

With empty vodka bottles

And his skin had turned a strange shade of yellow

Jaundice, my dad told me

It was the craziest thing I had ever heard

I mean, who would do that to themselves?

I didn't understand it when I was young

But as I get older

It's all beginning to make perfect sense...

## *DUI*

Ubers, Lifts, and

Driverless cars

Where were you when

My friend said—just one more

## A Guy Walks Into a Bar

July 17th, Houston Texas

A friend and I are getting day drunk

Why not?

A guy walks into the bar—

Hounds tooth jacket,

Check

Tweed vest,

Check

Bowtie,

Check

Handlebar mustache,

Check

Look it's Sherlock Holmes, I say

As the man sits down next to us

Are you English, I ask

I thought it was possible

An English country gentleman

Lost in the dregs of a big American city

He smiles,

Then—

More shots!

Are you a professor, I ask

He smiles again,

An actor perhaps

He smirks

Is he fucking with me, I wonder

How can a guy walk into a bar

In the middle of summer

In Houston Texas

Dressed like that,

And not expect questions

Is he a quack

An old hipster, who doesn't quite get it

Is he trying to make a statement

Well, okay

Here's your chance

I'm asking you

Say something

Don't you have anything to say

—silence—

Well then… Fuck You!

Suddenly,

The red-headed bartender turns banshee,

Pounds her fists upon the bar,

And in glorious ginger rage howls,

Get Out!!!

As we stumble out of the bar

Into the agony of the midday-sun

I turn to my friend and say—

I'm hungry

        I felt like Henry Chinaski

## When it Rains

When it rains I look at the grass

And the leaves on the trees

And the delicate pedals of flowers

And I see them drinking

Drinking

Drinking

And I hope they don't do what I do

And drink too much

## *Home*

It's nice to come inside

And sit next to the fire


With things, your things

Around you, and people


Who love you, they are

There too. And it's nice


Sometimes it's too nice

Because you know, you


Know you don't deserve

Nice things. You don't


Deserve love either,

not even a little bit


You look in the windows

Of the ones who do, and


You dream. And you drink

And you wonder why. But

You know why. You burned

Your house down the first

Chance you got.

## *Footloose Adonis*

He played Varsity Football

At a Chi-Town High School

Where he scored a touchdown

In the big championship game

When he joined the Navy

They sent him to

An old wooden sailing ship

Where he could primp and pose

For pictures with adoring tourist

They even gave him a medal for it!

He left the Navy a few years later

To go play college football

At a famous Division One school

In Florida

—But he didn't make it

He went to work at SeaWorld

And played baseball at a small

Community College instead

It was all downhill from there

But before his good looks faded

They got him a wife

Then the kids came

And a mortgage

Soon after that was the booze

And then the coke

I tried to help, we all did

But He was gone

A few years later, so were his feet

*Part 5*

## 40 Little Feets

Night fell upon Newtown on a chilly morning in December,

A day that everyone there will always remember

Principals, teachers, mothers, and wives

Young boys and girls with big playground eyes

Two to the chest, one to the head,

Bang-bang-bang, they were all dead

Nevermore the pitter-patter of 40 little feets,

Bouncing off the walls in the halls like joyful drumbeats

They sleep softly now under the dirt

Their bodies buried, but not the hurt

There were so many, but to name only a few:

Charlotte Bacon, the little ginger

In a pink dress and boots, what a hoot

James Mattitoli, everyone called him Jay,

He loved hamburgers and bacon,

But his mom's French Toast the most

Ana Marquez-Greene and her big grin

She is in heaven now,

But will surely smile when she sees her family again.

Caroline Previdi—silly Caroline,

And Madeleine Hsu, the shy girl who loved dogs,

I am sorry we couldn't protect you

The teachers tried, and many died,

But the gunman refused to yield

Poor kids, they should be playing outside,

Or coloring unicorns in their books,

Not lying in pools of blood at Sandy Hook

## *Nothing Ever Changes*

The wicked never change

Their black hearts bleeding

Venom and lies while

Deaf ears lay dying

On top hills of corpses

Madness piling upon madness

Until the whole world burns down

## *Tonight*

Tune up the guitar

Let's kill someone tonight

Open the jar, and eat it all

Candelabras and Vikings

Very, very frightening

Guns are half-price

At the dollar store

## Not Much

there is not much

left in the world

no God

no love

no kindness

just the ticking

of the clock

fearing death

we kill

laying waste to

anyone who ever

loved us

deaf to the screams

we hear nothing

feel nothing

do nothing

but clutch our crosses

and cry

## *Doughnut Shaded Sunsets*

I wish I could tell you the world

Was a happy place

Full of frolicking puppies

And doughnut shaded sunsets

But it's not

There is evil here

Who will hurt the ones you love

And while you wait for justice

They will hurt them again

And again

Until the son goes down

## *Songs...*

Some people are so lonely,

there are no songs for it.

Alone in their madness,

they weep.

Only the gadflies are on parade.

## Los Muertos

L.A. is dead man; I mean really dead.

I have never seen people so empty.

You can see it in their eyes as they

wander the aisles of the 99-cent stores

realizing that they can't afford to live.

You can see it in their faces

as they wait nervously at bus stops,

jumping at the shadows of their own

inhumanity.

They have had enough.

Enough of the Crips and Bloods,

enough of Jay Leno,

enough of the stale sunshine

and government cheese.

This is not what was promised.

There is no God here,

no jobs, or homes they can afford.

94

The best part of their day is when

they sit in motionless rivers of cars

and dream.


Not of angels or actors,

but about THE BIG ONE.

They hope it will save them,

just swallow them up.

They hope…

## Rain Dance

I listen to the rain dancing

across clay tile shingles

and try to imagine

the weight of it all.

The weight of water,

and shadows,

and light.

## The Wind

Wind is the only element in the natural world

That has been in all places

At all times

Over land and water

Night and day

Every second since the earth was born

Imagine the memories it carries

—And the souls that swirl in the dust

## The Dust

Into the dust we must go

We must We must We must

Toward the light

Or perpetual dark night

No one knows the truth

But only fools rush toward the light

## The Darkness

The Darkness
        Is merciful
The Darkness
        Forgives
The Darkness
        Knows everything
Everything
        That has ever been
Everything
        That ever will be
We are created
        In Darkness
We learn of our fears
        In Darkness
We discover our passions
        In Darkness
We commit our greatest sins
        In Darkness
And when the end comes,
        And it will
It is the Darkness
        The Immortal
The Immaculate
        Darkness
That will absolve us

*Part 6*

## Ebony Goddess

She was sweet and dark

Like the end of the world

## She Was...

The night we met

She was hoped up on ecstasy

And I was drunk

As a one-eyed pirate

So of course,

The sex was phenomenal

I couldn't tell you

What happened after that

But we managed

To run into each other again

A few years down the road

She was still brown and beautiful

And the sex was still amazing

In the morning I stood at the window

Smoking a cigarette

I asked her, what about us?

She laughed

Us? You aren't the serious type

She had me pegged all along

I liked her, she was alright

# *Morning Tea*

You like a cup of tea

Before your coffee

Then me

## *Sheets*

We lay on sweat soaked sheets

Our passions spent

Too tired to smile,

We breathe

## *Crazy Eyes*

You have

The most beautiful

Brown eyes

It's true

Everyone says so

But what they

Don't know,

What I will never

Tell them,

Is that your eyes

Change color

When you're wet

## ~~~Waves

Here you are again my love

Laying astride my salty shores

Giggling, as a thousand

Of my tiny tongues

Lap at your toes

Laughing, as my foamy froth

Caresses your feet

Gasping, as I surge upward

Between your thighs

And swirl swiftly

Around your waist

You cry out as I lift your breast

Like boats upon my tide,

And spray a million little kisses

Across your lips

You are afloat—we are one

Rising and falling,

Rising and falling,

My waves crashing

Forceful~~~yet tender

Against the beaches of your surrender

## *When The Rain Comes*

Your thighs tremble when the rain comes

Something in the sudden, swirling gust
Tingles your flesh

You feel the wetness before the first drop falls

When it comes, it comes hard
Pounding, unrelenting
It doesn't ask for permission

Just the way you like it

## *The Dom*

The ad said you were looking for a Dom

But I showed you

All you really needed was a man,

With a whip ~

## Manish Boy

I came home, masturbated,

Then called my girlfriend

And told her I was sorry

Not for that, for everything

Real men never say

They're sorry, she said

I know, I replied

As I put on a pair of

Her pink lace panties

And poured a glass of wine

A Merlot—her favorite.

## You u o ou uuu oo

Your ridiculously long neck

And gigantic nose

Are grossly out of proportion

With your Twizler thin limbs

And combat-boot laden feet

I would say you look funny

(If you weren't so damn sexy)

## La Petite Mort

La Petite Mort; Ah, Little Death.

Oh How I Yearn Your Blissful Heavens High,

In Lightness, Grasping, Gasping, Out of Breath,

My Spirit Soaring Upward as I Die.


Au Revoir; Expired to Darkness Rest,

In Coffin Prostrate Spent: Hell Awaits.

If Life Be Choice, I Choose Sweet Death Be Best,

Less Angels, Locked Behind Pearly Gates.


Mon Amour; My Risen Lover Calls.

With Sword to Battle, Against Which I Adore,

A Caesar, Laying Siege Upon Sovereign Walls.

Lay Impaled Upon My Blade, Dying, Yet MORE.

Yes, Yes, A Thousand, No—Ten!

Glory, Glory, To Die Inside You Again!

## *You, Again...*

You like to read books

Drink wine

And talk about your ex

As my tongue

Dances inside you

## *My Last Erection*

My Last erection, it's all I think about.

Really, I'm obsessed…

Dying doesn't bother me, that's easy.

Losing your manhood, that's hard.

Two balls and a cock, my holy trinity

It's all I've got

I'm worried about it. Will it come and go,

unappreciated like fleeting morning wood?

Will I accidently beat it to death, strangling

the life out of it as I did in my youth?

No!

I'm a man. I need a woman. I want a fist full

of hair and an aching wetness to take it all

as I blast out the last few drops of my humanity.

If there is justice in this world,

if there is a GOD,

that's the way it will be,

but it won't…

# Acknowledgements

Dreams: Originally published in *Poetry Quarterly* (Fall 2014)

Forty Little Feets, Waves, and Le Petite Mort: Originally published in *Dual Coast Magazine* Issue #2 (Summer 2014)

Road Trip: Originally published in *The Stray Branch* (Fall/Winter 2016)

Los Muertos: Originally published in *The Dime Show Review* Vol III (Summer 2017)

Rain Dance: Originally published in *Chronogram Magazine* (Jul 2018)

My Last Erection: Originally published in *The Los Angeles Review of Los Angeles* #13 (Summer 2018)

Songs: Originally published in *Harbinger Asylum* (Fall 2018)

The Day After: Originally published in *The River Poets Journal* Issue 2018 (Jan 2019)

Bukowski's Bungalow and Open Mic: Originally published in *The American Journal of Poetry* Vol. 6 (Jan 2019)

Morning Tea, and You Again: Originally published in *Peach Fuzz Magazine* (Oct 2019)

Guy Walks Into a Bar: Originally published in *Scars Publication's A Rose in The Dark* (May 2019), and Burning Bridges (Dec 2019)

Goodbye: Originally published in *Chronogram Magazine* (Dec 2019)

Picture Frame: Originally published in *Z Publication's California's Best Emerging Poets* (Dec 2019)

Metropolis: Originally published in *Transcendent Zero Press' Epiphanies of Love Anthology* (Feb 2019)

The Awkward Book: Originally published in *The Rio Grande Valley International Poetry Festival's Boundless Anthology* (Apr 2020)

Sweet Tea: Originally published in *Pure Slush Publishing's Growing Up Lifespan* Vol. 2 (Jun 2021)

My Heart: Originally published in HellBound Book's *Beautiful Tragedies II* Anthology (2021)

She Was: Originally published in *Sweetycat Press's Beautiful: In The Eye of The Beholder* Anthology (March 2022)

## About The Author

John Kojak is a Navy Veteran and graduate of The University of Texas who grew up in oily little towns around Houston, Texas during the Boom-and-Bust eras of the 1970's and 80's. He still lives there, with a nice woman and a mean cat. His poetry and short stories have appeared in a variety of books and magazines such as Poetry Quarterly, The American Journal of Poetry, California's Best Emerging Poets Anthology, Chronogram Magazine, Mystery Weekly, Switchblade Magazine, Pulp Modern, and many others.

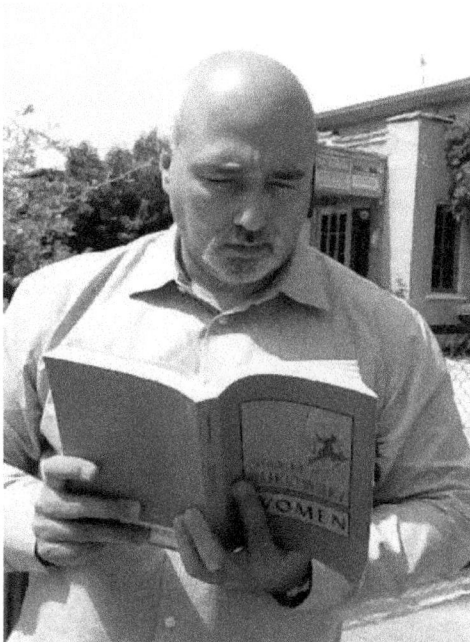